From Your Heart to Theirs

Delivering an Effective Sermon

PARTICIPANT'S GUIDE

Tony Franks
David Carroll

DISCIPLESHIP RESOURCES

P O BOX 340003 • NASHVILLE, TN 37203-0003
www.discipleshipresources.org

Thoughts on Teaching and Learning

Each one of us has a personal and unique learning style. It may be similar to that of others, but if we are able to use a learning style tailored to the way our brain recognizes, stores, and processes information, learning becomes easy and fun, and information is more effectively retained. Think of how you yourself prefer to learn. Perhaps you are a reader. Maybe you learn more easily and efficiently by listening in the form of music, sounds, or by voice. Perhaps you learn best in a 'hands-on' manner. If the teaching method suits your learning style, you can process and adapt any information quickly. Addressing the educational needs of all students during a session may require you to modify your presentation style.

While lecture alone is the least effective means of presenting material, group activity is one of the most effective. Relational activities in small groups, or sometimes in the larger class context, associate students with different learning styles and thereby offer a chance for the teacher to expose the students to multiple avenues of learning. Though some sessions will lend themselves to one or more specific learning styles, the instructor can use a combination to address the needs of the students. As teachers, we need to be creative!

Articles and guidelines concerning multiple intelligences refer to the research of Howard Gardner, or, the "eight ways of learning." These disciplines can be loosely grouped into three categories, or styles: auditory, visual, or tactile (also known as kinesthetic, as it can involve any form of participatory motion or perceived movement). Here are some activity suggestions:

Further help can be obtained in the 'Train the Trainers' section of the *Guidebook for Conference and District Directors* available from Discipleship Resources. You may also find these two books will spark your creativity:

Faithful Guides: Coaching Strategies for Church Leaders by Thomas Hawkins (DR465). Let coaching improve your creative teaching skills.

Always in Rehearsal: The Practice of Worship and the Presence of Children by James H. Ritchie, Jr. (DR427). Ritchie provides a helpful application of the multiple intelligences to the inclusion of all in corporate worship.

Auditory	Visual	Tactile
class discussion * show and tell creative rhythms and raps * debate * paraphrase or description * music * songs or rhymes * poetry * storytelling * reading * word games * seminars	charts and graphs * timeline * diagrams * cartoons * bulletin boards * photographs * videos * posters * journal writing * montages and collages * collections	games * simulations * puppets * sculpting * drama * dance * signing * construction * experiments * role-playing * origami * jig-saw puzzles

Contents

Goals for the Course

Session One
    Preparing Different Types of Sermons
    Reading vs. Memorizing vs. Extemporizing
    Seasons of the Christian Year

Session Two
    Your Story (A Personal Journey)
    Using the *United Methodist Hymnal*

Session Three
    Reading Aloud

    Storytelling
    Dealing with Fear
    Non-Verbal Language

Session Four
    Repeating a Sermon
    The Lay Speaker's Planning Sheet

Session Five
    Sermon Presentations

Suggested Reading and Information Sources
About the Authors

From Your Heart to Theirs: Delivering the Effective Sermon

GOALS FOR THE COURSE

To lead participants in preparing several kinds of sermons (topical, scriptural, personal narrative, etc.) by

- Providing plans for such—including worksheets

- Stressing the importance of good oral communication in preaching

- Offering further suggestions on incorporating stories and reading aloud

- Providing prayer and study time for revising

To evaluate this sermon based on specific criteria by

- Providing a videotape of the sermon

- Offering oral and written peer evaluations

- Providing instructor feedback on all areas

To offer additional related material by exploring

- Storytelling and reading aloud

- Using the *United Methodist Hymnal*

- Nonverbal communication

- Communicating with a host church

- Recommended reading list

[handwritten notes:] Revising of sermons to target your congregation

Know a hymn, prayer, + scripture + share it

3

Session One

This session will lead you through the steps in planning a sermon—three kinds of sermons, in fact:

- The sermon arising from Scripture (exegetical)

- The topical sermon

- The personal testimony

Each of these has similarities and differences, but all require careful, prayerful planning. Even the children's sermon, which will also be addressed in this session, needs careful planning. Every lay speaker needs a "quiver" or notebook of several kinds of sermons for use in short-term or long-term preaching. These include the kinds below as well as sermons for special occasions such as holidays (see the "Seasons of the Christian Year" below) or Laity Sunday.

THE SERMON ARISING FROM SCRIPTURE

This is the basic sermon, the one you will deliver if you use the lectionary or a favorite Scripture. It is called *exegetical*; that is, it exegetes, or "raises" a Scripture passage and leads an audience through an analysis of it. If you have a favorite Scripture passage, write it below (or write the lectionary passage for a Sunday coming up).

Read the Scripture several times: first quickly, then thoroughly in context, then prayerfully. As you *pray and reflect* on the Scripture, *write down your ideas* for a possible sermon in your notebook. Be sure to stay focused on exegesis, not *isogesis (what we want the passage to say).* Try asking these questions:

- What do you think it meant to its first hearers?

- What might it say to you and others?

- What does it call you to do?

- If you were to take it very seriously, what life changes would it require?

Then, and only then, you should *consult other resources*, commentaries, Bible dictionaries, cross-references, and other illustrations. Take careful notes; you may change your ideas, so write down any thoughts in your notebook.

> The Board of Discipleship <www.gbod.org>, the United Methodist Church <www.umc.org>, and The Upper Room <www.upperroom.org> all have websites with links to sermon helps.

Your next step is to *define with crystal clarity* exactly what it is you want to say and why, and for what response you are calling. It's a good idea to write this out and keep it in front of you as you work. What response might you call for as a result of the above Scripture?

Keeping the main idea and purpose in mind will also help you to *narrow your ideas* and resources.

Organize your ideas in a manner that best suits your style, your message, and your intended listeners. A good fact to keep in mind at this point is this: The organization of a sermon is a definite persuasive element.

[handwritten: what the Scripture reads]

What you say in closing is of utmost importance. This idea is called the "law of recency," which means that an audience remembers

[handwritten: Children's Sermon are hardest] 4 *[handwritten: Lay Speakers must be Students of the Bible]*

longest what it hears last. *Write out your concluding statement*—and plan to use it. Finally, *write a complete manuscript of your sermon*—whether or not you plan to use the manuscript as you deliver the sermon.

THE TOPICAL SERMON

This kind of sermon allows lay speakers to address issues and ideas from their own experience, interest, training, or profession. List some of your interests (professional or otherwise) below.

_____

_____

Although this method is usually most interesting to the beginning lay speaker, it does have some pitfalls and carries with it some cautions:

- Some lay speakers tend to keep coming back to the same topic over and over. Audiences may begin to predict that they will hear a "same song, second verse" kind of sermon. Can you recall any of these?

- There is a tendency to get too wrapped up in one's own emotions. Has that ever happened to you?

- It is easy to fall into the trap of using inappropriate Scripture choices—or too many Scriptures in one sermon. Have you ever heard one of those?

- A lay speaker, especially a guest, is generally not in the position to deal with controversial subjects. Why is this true?

Preparation for this kind of sermon requires the same careful consideration of topic, congregation make-up, and reflection. The steps in

preparation are basically the same, but the selection of Scripture may be moved further "down the list." That is, the Scripture selection may come as a result of recall, from studying a concordance, or even from the suggestion of a hymn phrase or title. (Using the hymnal is covered in Session Two.)

The topical sermon also needs careful organization as well as a clear purpose. Very careful examination of Scripture is necessary, however, to be absolutely certain that it says what you "want it to say." Using a Scripture out of context simply because it has the "topic word" in it is ill advised. A good Bible dictionary or another translation of the selected Scripture can help to avoid poor use of a Scripture reference.

Be sure to consider the Scripture in context. Look at what goes before and comes after the selection you want to use. Ask these questions:

- Who is speaking, and to whom?

- What is the setting, the situation, or the conflict?

- How do you think the first hearers reacted?

- What do you think was the desired response from the original speaker?

- Would your desired response be the same?

How could you use your own experience in a topical sermon? What response might you seek from an audience as a result?

THE PERSONAL TESTIMONY

Although this particular method is detailed in Session Two, some similarities to the other two kinds of sermon need to be pointed out. This

Get a good Bible dictionary 5 *3 different translations*
"Vine's" + a Commentary; use a Hymnal *Living Bible God News English Bible*

kind of sermon gives lay speakers an opportunity to share their faith journey so that others may benefit from their experience, example, or even mistakes.

The personal testimony requires the same kind of preparation and reflection; it can also call for a response. Of special importance is the way one connects one's story with the audience and the Church's larger story. For example, do you identify with David, with Peter, with Martha, or even with blind Bartimaeus? Do you feel like John Wesley or even Susannah Wesley sometimes? How about the elder son in the parable? How does your personal testimony compare with the life stories of the people to whom you are speaking?

While every lay speaker needs to have a personal testimony (even versions of varying lengths) in the "quiver" of sermons, pitfalls still exist: preaching too much of the same idea or seeming to be too self centered (or perhaps self-effacing). *Should fit into whole ine theleme*

Be sure to take some time to work through the section "Finding Your Story" in this workbook. *Testimony is your walk w/ The Lord*

THE CHILDREN'S SERMON

The children's sermon may be the most difficult to "preach" for several reasons:

- It requires careful consideration of the age and life stage of the children in the audience.

- It requires knowledge of children's attention span.

- It requires careful attention to feedback from the children.

- It requires the ability to adjust one's ideas, words, examples, and plans—even one's purpose.

- It requires the ability to laugh at one's self.

- It requires one to remember that the adults are listening too.

The children's sermon is not just an impromptu two-minute entertainment. Children remember what you say and do, as well as how you say and do it. Furthermore, children are good at memorizing and enjoy memorizing short Scripture verses, songs, and mottoes. When planning the children's sermon, try writing your main idea in a simple sentence for children to memorize. Plan to repeat it several times during the sermon.

A simple message using an object is often the best kind for children. A toy or trick engages their attention and can be related to an idea such as love or forgiveness or kindness.

One of the most successful children's sermons we have seen is "The Box." This method uses a wooden box that a child can take home and bring back with an object she or he chooses. The speaker then uses the object for a sermon. "The Box" takes real practice and self-confidence, but even the adults in the congregation eagerly anticipate "Box Time." What would you do if a precocious child brought the box and when you opened it there was nothing there? What would your message be?

It is always a good idea for the lay speaker to ask if the children's sermon is his or her responsibility—and be prepared—just in case.

What are some objects you could carry in your pocket or a small bag to use for children's sermons?

READING VS. MEMORIZING VS. EXTEMPORIZING

What is the best method for delivering a sermon? Should you read from a manuscript? Should you memorize word for word? Or should you use notes for reminders? Each method has advantages and disadvantages.

Reading from a Manuscript

Advantages

- It is precise and easily controlled.

- There is little danger of forgetting.

- It may be more comfortable for some beginning speakers.

Disadvantages

- Poor reading may destroy the effect.

- It allows little eye contact and may result in lack of audience response.

- Shuffling pages or losing pages can be distracting.

Memorizing a Manuscript

Advantages

- It allows more eye contact, freedom of movement, and gesturing.

- There is little margin for error in content.

- It may seem more natural to the listeners.

Disadvantages

- It sometimes results in a stilted, monotonous delivery.

- The speaker risks forgetting a part of the sermon.

- It allows very little room for variation.

Extemporizing (Using Notes and Memory)

Advantages

- Organization may be clearer than in other types.

- It allows some freedom for variation.

- It allows good eye contact and freedom of movement.

Disadvantages

- It is difficult to stay within a particular time limit.

- Some speakers read the notes and little else.

- Overconfidence sometimes leads to loss of the train of thought.

So, which method is best? The choice depends on the speaker. Some are good readers; others have good memories. Still others find that remembering the points requires little more than a set of notes. The lay speaker should try several methods to determine which works best for him or her—and for the audience.

Seasons of the Christian Year

SEASON	COLOR	MEANING OF THE SEASON
Advent	Purple and/or Blue	Waiting and expectation for God's coming as Jesus the Babe
Christmas	White and Gold	Celebration of God's being with us through Jesus
Season after Epiphany	Green	Celebration of the ways God became known to the whole world in Jesus
Lent	Purple	Season in which we prepare and remember the suffering of Christ

Holy Week
  Palm Sunday
  Maundy Thursday
  Good Friday
	
	Purple or Red
	Purple or Red
	No color or Black
		Remembrance of the final week of Jesus' earthly life, including his triumphal entry, the Last Supper, and the Passion of Christ

Easter	Gold and White	Celebration of the resurrection of Jesus
Pentecost	Red	Celebration of the birth of the Church and the Holy Spirit's sending the Church into the world
Season after Pentecost (Ordinary Time)	Green	We learn about the kingdom of God through Jesus' teachings and miracles.

Session Two

FINDING YOUR STORY: A PERSONAL JOURNAL

We all have a story to tell, and often an important part of our witness as lay speakers involves relating stories of our personal journey of faith. This journal activity will help you to put together your story for other people to hear. Use this form as a guide, adding more if you need to.

Categories

Is your story mainly about a *person,* an *event,* another *sermon* you've heard, a special *hymn,* or *something else*? Think about it and write it below.

_____

_____

_____

Expanding the Subject

There are three areas to pursue here. (If you need more space, use a notebook or journal.)

1. What makes this subject important to you?

_____

_____

_____

2. How is it similar to or different from other related subjects? What makes it special?

_____

_____

_____

3. How did it affect you?

_____

_____

_____

Making Connections

Close your eyes and think about your subject. Try to remember exactly what you saw, heard—even touched, smelled, or tasted. Write it down.

1. Sights, sounds, tastes, smells, etc.

_____

_____

_____

2. Now try to describe exactly how you felt, your emotions. ("It was as if . . . .")

_____

_____

_____

Making It Their Story

Go back and look over all you've written so far. Then answer these questions:

1. Why would you want to share this story?

_____

_____

_____

2. What would make your hearers interested in hearing your story?

_____

_____

_____

3. With what parts of the story could your audience most identify?

_____

_____

_____

4. What *don't* they know that you might need to tell them?

_____

_____

_____

5. What is the most important part of the story?

_____

_____

_____

Calling for Their Response

This is most important, because effective organization of ideas is one of your most powerful tools. The material should be organized so that it leads to the response you wish to have from the hearers.

1. What do you need to tell them first? How will you introduce the subject?

_____

_____

_____

2. Will you develop this as a narrative, a series of ideas, a description of a place or person, or something else? List the parts in order. (If this is a narrative, your details will fall into a "time" order; you will relate a sequence of events. If this is to be descriptive, your details will fall into a "space" order: you will become something like a camera to your audience.)

_____

_____

_____

3. How do you want hearers to respond? What do you need to say to help them?

_____

_____

_____

Looking Back

You've taken a journey, and you've considered taking others on the journey with you. You've looked at their needs, and you've made a decision about what you want them to do, feel, or see as a result. Read over what you've written, and then think about the questions below.

1. What Scripture passages come to mind as you read? (If there are no particular verses, what key words?)

_____

_____

_____

_____

2. What hymns or phrases of hymns came to mind?

_____

_____

_____

3. Write an introduction to your story below.

_____

_____

_____

4. Finally, write your conclusion, including the part that asks for a response, below.

_____

_____

_____

You now have an outline of "your story." You probably need more paper to put down all the details you've thought of, so it's time to do just that. Then, using the material above, put together a complete manuscript.

Try it out on a hearer; read it to someone else; or have someone read it aloud to you. Discard parts or add more if you need to. Good speechmaking, like good writing, demands revision. And remember, most of Jesus' stories were brief. Put it together in its best order—then *tell your story*.

USING THE UNITED METHODIST HYMNAL

In the previous activity you relived part of your journey of faith, and during that time you probably found yourself humming a familiar hymn or two. Singing—even from the time of the Wesleys—has been a very important part of our lives as Christians and as Methodists. In the space below write the name of one of your favorite hymns.

_____

_____

_____

Now look it up in *The United Methodist Hymnal*. Write the number here. _____

Who wrote the words, and when were they written?

_____

_____

Who wrote the tune, and when was it written?

_____

_____

What is the tune name?

_____

What does the hymn say to you? In other words, why is it important to you?

_____

_____

_____

The questions you have just answered illustrate the one reason the hymnal is important to you as a lay speaker. It contains the inspired words of writers from centuries past as well as those of today. These words have been comfort, creed, and cheer to Christians for years. Yet, there is more to the United Methodist Hymnal than hymns. There are psalms, prayers, guides for worship settings, and many other references. The activities in this session are designed to help you see the organization of the hymnal, some of the kinds of information you will find in it, and methods for using the hymnal as a source for sermon and worship planning.

If you look at the opening pages of the hymnal, you will see that it is divided into several sections. Look for these headings and thumb through the material found under each one:

- General Services

- Hymns, Canticles & Acts of Worship

- Psalter

- Other General Services & Acts of Worship

- Indexes

Because of the limitations of this session, it is impossible to look closely into each of these sections, but some explanation about three is in order before investigation of hymns and the Psalter.

General Services Sections

Quite often you as a lay speaker will be called upon to do more than just preach. You will be responsible for planning a service for a particular occasion, such as a mid-week prayer service, a brief worship service in a setting other than the church, or even a whole Sunday morning worship service. The litanies in these sections give standard designs for services, and if they are used along with the *United Methodist Book of Worship* (*UMBOW*), will provide invaluable help for organizing a meaningful service for almost any occasion.

Indexes

Look first at the **Index of Topics and Categories** on page 934. This index is a quick reference to general and specific themes and occasions. For instance, if you were looking for a hymn to use in a service of assurance and blessing, your first inclination might be just to use "Blessed Assurance," but a closer look will open even more treasures. Look under the heading "Calmness and Serenity" and write the name of an unfamiliar hymn. (Note: Try to avoid always using the same familiar hymns.) Write the name of it below.

_____

_____

If you skipped right over "Thy Holy Wings, O Savior" (502) and "Heal Me, Hands of Jesus" (262), go back and look at them. Whether you know the tune is not particularly important, though they both have lovely melodies that are easy to sing. Not only are they easy, singable prayers for healing and safety, they could be used as unison readings.

That index is easy enough to use. Just remember that the index also lists prayers as well as hymns. Prayers and poetry are listed in italic type. Try a few more subjects, and use the same method as suggested above. Even reading the words to a familiar hymn before using it is always a good idea. For example, what do the words to "Break Thou the Bread of Life" (599) really say?

_____

_____

_____

If you are planning a service around a particular Scripture selection, or if you need more inspiration for your sermon, take a look at the **Index of Scripture: Hymns, Canticles, Prayers & Poems** on page 924. Here you will find hymns referenced by Scripture, although it is not a good idea to limit the selection to those listed. Very often, reading through some of the suggested hymns will call to mind others that might more clearly augment the message of your sermon. Knowing exactly what you want your listeners to do as a result of your message will also help to determine your hymn selection.

Try this: If you wanted to help them to understand the working of the Holy Spirit, how could the hymn "Holy Spirit, Come Confirm Us" (331) be used?

_____

_____

_____

Here is another. Read the verses of "Help Us Accept Each Other" (560). What does it call us to do?

_____

_____

_____

If you liked those words, go to another index for more hymns by Fred Kaan. Look at the **Index of Composers, Arrangers, Authors, Translators, and Sources** on page 914. List two other hymns by Fred Kaan and tell what they say to us as modern Christians.

_____

_____

_____

_____

_____

In this index, you can find hymns by your favorite writers and composers. How many hymns do we have listed by the following?

Charles Wesley   _____

Fred Pratt Green   _____

Jane Marshall   _____

Read some of them—as you would a passage of Scripture. Does a passage of Scripture come to mind?

Suppose a passage of Scripture does come to mind. You already know how to prepare a sermon based on Scripture, make a note of these hymns for later use.

The **Metrical Index** is not as confusing as it might look at first. Simply put, this index lists hymns that have the same meter—or number of syllables per line. Of course, the listings are by tune name; that is, the name of the music, not the words. One advantage of this index for the lay speaker who is also planning a service is that it sometimes allows the use of new hymns to older, more familiar tunes. Here is one example:

The meter for each verse of "Amazing Grace" (378) is CM, common meter, or 8.6.8.6 (a line of eight syllables followed by one of six syllables, then the same pattern repeated). Use your fingers and say the words; it is simple. Now, what if you really wanted to use the grand words to "Forgive Our Sins as We Forgive" (390), but nobody had time to learn the tune DETROIT? Because it has the same meter as "Amazing Grace" (CM), everybody can sing it to that tune.

Your instructor has other activities for using the hymns, Psalter, and other treasures of the United Methodist Hymnal. Remember, next to the Bible, the hymnal is your most important source of information and inspiration.

Session Three

This session is about reading aloud, story-telling, dealing with stage fright, non-verbal communication, and some of the paperwork of lay speaking assignments.

READING ALOUD

If you think of all the speakers whom you enjoy hearing, you will find that most of them are not only good storytellers, but also good readers. Their voices put you into another setting, and you wait eagerly for the climax of the story. How do we as lay speakers improve our ability to read aloud and to tell stories? Practice helps, but it must be the right kind of practice. Very few of us have the voice of James Earl Jones or our first grade teacher, but we can adopt some of their methods.

Here are some reading assignments to look at, along with a story and several suggestions for improving the ability to tell a good story.

"Reading Practice I" is from Psalm 133. Read it through and think about what it says.

What is the main idea of the text? What is the tone or mood?

_____

_____

_____

Which words are the most important? Write them here.

_____

_____

This passage has been formatted for easier reading. That is, the lines end at places in the text where pauses or complete stop would be helpful. (See note below.)

The indentions are placed to group main ideas or idea sequences together. Practice reading the selection aloud and pausing at the ends of main ideas.

Reading Practice I

Psalm 133:1-3

How very good and pleasant it is
    when kindred live together in unity!
It is like the precious oil on the head,
    running down upon the beard,
    on the beard of Aaron,
    running down over the collar of his robes.
It is like the dew of Hermon,
    which falls on the mountains of Zion.
For there the LORD ordained his blessing,
    life forevermore.

Here's a suggestion for marking pauses on your paper

- Use one slash / for a very slight pause, for example, in many places where there is a comma in the text.

- Use two slashes // for a full-stop pause, for example, where there's a question or sentence ending.

- Use three slashes /// to mark a dramatic pause, for example, when there's a rhetorical question. (Caution: Don't overdo this one!)

One of the marks of a very good reader is the way she or he stresses certain words and "unstresses" others. For instance, short words such as *the*, *a*, *so*, *and*, and *it*, as well as most prepositions, are generally shortened. (In the first verse of Reading Practice I, the words that should not be stressed are *and*, *it*, and *in*. Try it.)

Really good readers also make an extra effort to pronounce final consonants—unless, of course, the following word begins with the same consonant. (For example, you cannot pronounce the end consonant and the initial consonant in this phrase without sounding really affected: *Tom must not trip Peter.*)

Look over the selection and see where final consonants need to be practiced.

There are some consonants that need special mention. These are /l/, /m/, /n/, and /ŋ/. A very slight elongation of these will give the voice more resonance. (The /ŋ/ sound is what we hear at the ends of words such as *bring*, *long*, and *doing*.)

Finally, read the selection to see whether there are words that are unfamiliar, or that might be unfamiliar to an audience (*Aaron*, *Hermon*?). A good reader will know exactly how to pronounce all the words—and will have a good idea of what each one means.

So here is your checklist for reading any selection. Try to use this list for any selection you will be reading before an audience.

☐ Where should brief pauses occur? Are there any dramatic pauses?

☐ What words need to be unstressed?

☐ Where do you see final letters that need to be pronounced for clarity?

☐ What words contain resonators (/l/, /m/, /n/, or /ŋ/)?

☐ What words might cause problems for a first-time hearer?

Below is another selection, one that is probably familiar to you. Read it—and record it, if possible—and then try the suggestions above before you read it and record it again.

Reading Practice II

Romans 12:1-8

I appeal to you therefore, brothers and sisters, by the mercies of God, to present your bodies as a living sacrifice, holy and acceptable to God, which is your spiritual worship. Do not be conformed to this world, but be transformed by the renewing of your minds, so that you may discern what is the will of God—what is good and acceptable and perfect.

For by the grace given to me I say to everyone among you not to think of yourself more highly than you ought to think, but to think with sober judgment, each according to the measure of faith that God has assigned. For as in one body we have many members, and not all the members have the same function, so we, who are many, are one body in Christ, and individually we are members one of another. We have gifts that differ according to the grace given to us: prophecy, in proportion to faith; ministry, in ministering; the teacher, in teaching; the exhorter, in exhortation; the giver, in generosity, the leader, in diligence; the compassionate, in cheerfulness.

Notes on reading this passage:

_____

_____

_____

STORYTELLING AND USING ILLUSTRATIONS

When Jesus taught, he taught with parables; that is, he told stories to illustrate the point he was trying to make. (For an excellent explanation of Jesus' use of parables, refer to William Barclay's *The Daily Bible Study Series: The Gospel of Matthew*, vol. 2, pp. 53ff.) Good lay speakers should also use illustrations that convey their message. In the story below we see a humble figure who becomes the hero of the story, a method similar to one Jesus often used: an ironic twist in the conclusion.

Christ Ain't Got No Church Here

Like many small towns, Winona is built along a railroad. In Winona, Front Street runs parallel to the railroad, with the older stores facing the depot. At the north end of Front Street, sitting perpendicular—on Magnolia Street—is Garner Service Station. Here my father-in-law, Barksdale Garner, ran a gas station for more than sixty years. During those sixty years he watched the town change, and observed the people of the town; and during these years he became a master storyteller. I want to tell you one of his stories.

There was a man named Ben who drove a dray wagon from the depot to the businesses in town. He knew where everybody lived and a little about how they lived. One day a man got off the train—it was a Sunday train, and not many people were stirring—and stood looking up and down Front Street. The stores certainly weren't open, but Ben had met the train, and the man asked him, "Can you tell me where to find a Church of Christ?"

Ben removed his hat. "Sir?"

"The Church of Christ. I'm looking for a Church of Christ."

Ben scratched his head and looked up the street, then down. Then he pointed up Magnolia Street. "Now up there is the Methodist; that's Mr. Harrison's church. And over yonder is the Baptist; that's Mr. Davis' church."

"No, I'm looking for the Church of Christ."

Ben rested his hat on his knee and thought some more. "Well, now, across from the Baptist is the Presbyterian; that's Mr. Hawkins' church."

"But I'm looking for a Church of Christ."

"I tell you that's about all, but up on the end of the this street is the Episcopal; that's Mr. Dumas' church." The man insisted on finding the Church of Christ.

Ben put his hat back on, clicked his mule, and started away. "Sir," he said, turning back, "I don't reckon Christ got a church in this town."

Here are some suggestions for storytellers.

- Good storytellers often give someone else credit for the story. Mark Twain and Edgar Allan Poe did it. The teller of the story above did it. Giving someone else credit sets the speaker apart and lends a different kind of interest to the story.

- Separate yourself from the story, unless it's about you. There's a section in this course about telling your own story.

- Create a setting; put your listeners in a *place*. Notice that the story above has a specific time and place. If you use "canned" stories or illustrations, check the date. Is the story timeless? Does it fit?

- Use non-verbal language to delineate the characters: focus on a separate direction for each character. Simply shifting the eyes or slightly moving the head is usually enough.

- Avoid the use of dialect unless you are a real expert; changing one or two words will create the same effect. And never use hints of dialect in an offensive manner.

- Avoid stories that are questionable, those that might make someone uncomfortable. If you are in doubt, don't use the story.

- Be sure the story fits the speaker, the audience, and the occasion.

Notes on storytelling:

_____

_____

_____

_____

_____

DEALING WITH FEAR

Everyone has a certain amount of stage fright; in fact, some stage fright keeps a speaker alert. Two results can come from stage fright:

1. If there is too much, a speaker can "freeze up" and forget all or part of the presentation.

2. If there is too little, a speaker can become over-confident and *forget all or part of the presentation!*

Some of the symptoms of stage fright are "butterflies in the stomach," trembling knees, and sweaty palms. Some methods of dealing with these symptoms are these:

- Realize that they may occur and anticipate them.

- Remember that they bother the speaker much more than they do the audience.

- Prepare thoroughly. Few things give more confidence to a speaker.

- Take a few minutes before the presentation for centering, deep breathing, and prayer.

- Remember that the Holy Spirit is there during the presentation.

Some speakers reveal their nervousness by clearing the throat, putting hands into pockets, jingling pocket change, or adjusting hair. All of these—and anything else that causes a distraction—should be avoided.

NON-VERBAL LANGUAGE

Non-verbal language is any message or signal a speaker sends to an audience without using words. For instance, a speaker who shifts her weight from one foot to the other or constantly grips the lectern may send the message, "I'm really nervous." A speaker who keeps his arms folded in front may send a message of determination and defiance.

In addition to posture and stance, clothing and hair can also send a message. The speaker who is well dressed and well groomed sends a message of care and credibility. That is, the audience is assured that she or he is sincere and thoughtful enough of the audience to prepare the appearance as well as the mind.

Proximity to the audience also sends a distinct message. A speaker who moves from behind the lectern or pulpit may seem to be saying, "I'm putting this speech on a personal level; I'm talking to you one-on-one." A speaker who remains behind the lectern all the time presents a more formal approach to speaking. A good speaker will use variety in proximity.

Look at the following examples. What non-verbal message does each one send?

1. A middle-aged woman, whose accessories include *haute couture* shoes and expensive gold bracelets, also wears a tailored beige silk suit with a designer scarf. She paces back and forth, pointing at particular members of the audience as she speaks.

   _____

   _____

2. A pretty teenager dressed in a sweater and low-rise jeans speaks softly to a group of adults, but looks at her notes instead of the audience.

   _____

   _____

3. A sixtyish, well-dressed distinguished man in rimless glasses grips the lectern with both hands and gestures only with nods of his head and movements of his eyes.

   _____

   _____

(Actually, this describes President Franklin D. Roosevelt, who could stand only with support. He mastered the art of effective gestures using only his shoulders and head.)

4. A man of about thirty-five, dressed casually in a sweater, khaki pants, and loafers speaks to an audience about his work with prisoners. As he speaks, he gestures with an upward, open-palm movement and glances occasionally at his notes.

   _____

   _____

Audiences expect people of different ages, sexes, and backgrounds to use different postures and gestures. How might the non-verbal language of a retired preacher differ from that of a high-school student selling yearbook ads? What kinds of non-verbal language would you expect from these: a kindergarten teacher, a convenience store clerk, a funeral director, a garage mechanic, a traffic cop, a bank loan officer? How is each appropriate? How might each one of the above carry over natural non-verbal language in a public speaking environment?

   _____

   _____

   _____

   _____

EXAMPLES OF NON-VERBAL LANGUAGE

Action	Signal
Reading in a monotone	Lack of preparation
Looking away from the audience	Uncertainty, shyness
Forced, repetitive gestures	Insincerity, amateurishness
Feet set solidly on floor	Confidence
Smiling	Friendliness, security
Removing glasses or stepping in front of lectern	"Let's get down to business."
Overdressing ("power clothes")	"I'm better than you are."
Open posture	Acceptance
Open palm toward audience	"Stop!" or "Wait!"
Palms up, arms outstretched	Asking, pleading, welcoming

Session Four

This session is designed to address individual problems and to give you help on any area you feel needs more attention. In order to better discover your needs, go back to the sheet you received in the mail out titled "Sermon and Participant Information." Your instructor will give you an extra copy to hand in just before you make your presentation so that he or she can make written suggestions. It might be helpful to walk through the questions as an example.

THE SERMON TITLE

Your sermon needs a title that piques the imagination and gives hints about your topic. "Don't Lose Your Enjoyment" is a title taken from advice given to me in Zimbabwe by my driver when we discovered that the bus had left me. I used it with a sermon about encouragement. You need not worry too much in the beginning about a title; often a phrase from Scripture or from a hymn will come to you.

Be sure to avoid titles that are too cute or titles that make an empty promise of an exciting sermon. Your listeners may remember—and even talk about—your title, but they will remember little that you actually said.

SCRIPTURE REFERENCES

There's a word or two of caution here also. Too many Scripture references are difficult for your hearers to follow. Stick to one or two, and be sure to use them in context.

SUPPORT AND ILLUSTRATIONS

This material has been covered, but if you plan to tell a story, writing it out rather than relying completely on memory is a good idea. Often in writing you can discover a better way to tell it. (See the material in the session on storytelling.)

RESPONSE FROM HEARERS

If you don't know what you want your hearers to do or feel as a result of your delivery, they certainly won't know what to do. Imagine a listener coming up to you after your presentation and saying, "So what?" How would you respond?

FAVORITES AND SUCH

Some people really enjoy reading and taking notes. For others, this is almost an unnatural act; they are visual people. Some pianists enjoy practicing scales; others would rather just "play." However, each part is necessary, and a disciplined sermon preparation complete with prayer and study will produce a meaningful sermon.

Some people really enjoy selecting hymns. I'm one of those. Even when I listen to a sermon, I'm thinking, "I know a hymn that says just that." Studying the inspired words of hymn writers will help you to augment your sermon.

REPEATING A SERMON

Repeating a sermon may not be as simple as it seems. Why? Because no two audiences are the same. The speaker who takes manuscript in hand to the second audience without first evaluating the sermon and the new audience is stepping into dangerous territory. No two audiences come together with the same background, the same knowledge, or the same interests. A sermon that elicited hugs and smiles at a home church might get a lukewarm response somewhere else.

Not only does the audience change, but the speaker also changes. How have you changed since you presented your first sermon? Go back and look at it, or ask someone who did not hear it the first time to look at it. In what ways are you different now? Have fresh ideas about the subject arisen? Have you had an experience that emphasizes the main point—or another point? What needs to be changed?

In the space below write down some of the concerns you have about your sermon preparation and discuss them with members of your group.

_____

_____

_____

_____

Now write down some of the responses or solutions you were offered.

_____

_____

_____

_____

If you are using this workbook in a lay speaking course, this is your last meeting together before you assemble to present your sermons. Take another look at the evaluation questions on the following page. Pray for yourself and for each other. Listen openly and respond in the same way you want others to respond to you.

On the following page you will find a planning guide for times when you are called upon to fill the pulpit at a guest church. Feel free to duplicate it and use it when necessary. Having it completed for each presentation will make your visit more comfortable, both for you as well as for the host church.

LAY SPEAKER'S PLANNING SHEET

Church/Charge_____

Location _____Phone _____

Date of Presentation(s) _____ Time(s) _____

Directions:

Contact Person (at sites)_____

Where to meet _____Time _____

Suggested topic _____

Parts of Service or Event   *Who Is Responsible*

Bulletin information you are to provide (sermon title, hymns, etc.). Needed by (date)
_____

Congregational description:

Biographical information requested? Photo? _____

Contacted by _____ Date_____

Session Five

This is the session in which you are to present your sermon. As a reminder, here are the questions that will be asked of each participant. Keep these questions and use them as you prepare and deliver other sermons. Remember to respond with love!

1. What did you hear as the main idea of the presentation?

_____

_____

_____

_____

2. At what point did you feel most "connected to" this message?

_____

_____

_____

_____

3. What did you feel that the speaker wanted the audience to do as a result of hearing this message?

_____

_____

_____

_____

4. How would you describe the speaker's best quality?

_____

_____

_____

_____

5. What could the speaker do next time that would help you or other listeners?

_____

_____

_____

_____

Additional Comments:

_____

_____

_____

_____

_____

_____

_____

Suggested Reading and Information Sources

Benedict, Dan, and Craig Miller. *Contemporary Worship for the 21st Century: Worship or Evangelism?* Nashville: Discipleship Resources, 1994.

Bone, David L., and Mary J. Scifres. *The United Methodist Music and Worship Planner*. Nashville: Abingdon Press. (Available each year.)

Craddock, Fred B. *Preaching*. Nashville: Abingdon Press, 1985.

Craddock, Fred B., edited by Mike Graves and Richard Ward. *Craddock Stories*. St. Louis: Chalice Press, 2001.

Elliott, Mark Barger. *Creative Styles of Preaching*. Louisville: Westminster John Knox Press, 2000.

Foster, Richard J. *Celebration of Discipline: The Path to Spiritual Growth* (Revised Edition). San Francisco: Harper San Francisco, div. Of Harper Collins Publishers, 1988.

Hickman, Hoyt L. *Worshiping with United Methodists: A Personal Inventory Method*. Nashville: Abingdon Press, 1996.

Kinghorn, Kenneth Cain. *Discovering Your Spiritual Gifts*. Grand Rapids: Zondervan Publishing House, 1981.

Kinghorn, Kenneth Cain. *Gifts of the Spirit*. Nashville: Abingdon Press, 1976.

Swears, Thomas R. *Preaching to Head and Heart*. Nashville: Abingdon Press, 2000.

Webb, Joseph M. *Preaching Without Notes*. Nashville: Abingdon Press, 2001.

_____

_____

_____

_____

_____

_____

_____

About the Writers

Tony Franks, organist, pianist, and former Certified Lay Speaker in the Mississippi United Methodist Conference, has served as president of the Mississippi Chapter of the Fellowship of United Methodists in Music and Worship Arts. He is a retired teacher of music, writing, English, and oral communication. An ordained elder in the PCUSA, he currently fills the pulpit at First Presbyterian Church (USA) in Grenada, MS.

He has led lay speaking courses in the Mississippi Conference, Lake Junaluska UM Assembly and at Africa University, Harare. He has written and led other courses on use of the hymnal for the UMC as well as the St. Andrew and Mississippi Presbyteries and for the Alabama/Mississippi Presbyterian Women.

His Sunday School lessons have been published in the Mississippi UM *Advocate* and the South Carolina UM *Advocate*.

Rev. David Carroll, Senior Pastor at Alta Woods United Methodist Church in Jackson, MS, was ordained an elder in the North Mississippi Conference in 1985, and served pastoral appointments in Corinth, Columbus, and Winona. Eight years at Galloway church in Jackson followed before David moved to the Alta Woods church in 2006.

A 1978 graduate of Millsaps College in Jackson, David received the Master of Divinity degree at Emory University's Candler School of Theology.

He enjoys tennis, backpacking, guitar, canoeing, golf, and his family—his wife Laura, their son Benjamin, and daughters Kathryn and Mary Evelyn.

ACKNOWLEDGEMENTS

In 1998, when Gay Huff, MS Conference Director of Lay Speaking Ministries, first approached me about heading a committee to design a course for lay speakers who wanted to hone their speaking skills, she had CLS Pam Thompson in mind to help. Meeting along with David Carroll and me, Pam offered valuable input on the kinds of material needed for this course as well as perception into feedback from those who took the course as she and I led it for the Mississippi Conference.

In July 2001, Tim Moss of the General Board of Discipleship in Nashville; Dr. Evelyn Laycock, Director of the Lay Ministry Center at Lake Junaluska Assembly, NC; and Leslie Heaton, SC Director of Lay Speaking Ministries, expressed interest in my developing some of the material into a course that could be published and used by other teachers in districts and conferences across the country. The *Instructor's Guide* and *Participant Workbook* that David Carroll and I have prepared are the result of their confidence and encouragement.

Finally, thanks are due to the many participants from diverse backgrounds who have offered kind comments about the course. These participants—lawyers, truck drivers, professors, retired teachers, and everyday people—want to do more than just "fill a pulpit." They want to do the best job they can to bring the word of God to the people of God.

Tony Franks
January 2002